VOLCANOES

GREGORY VOGT

Franklin Watts
New York/Chicago/London/Sydney
A First Book

VOLCANOES

Photographs copyright ©:
Photo Researchers/Soames Summer & Hayes 4K8767, cover; J.D. Griggs/U.S. Geological Survey, 1, 48; Culver Pictures, 8, 10 (top); The Bettman Archive, 10 (bottom); E.R. Degginger/Earth Scenes, 14, 23; NPS/Weatherstock, 17; Otto Hahn/Peter Arnold, Inc., 18; James D. Watt/Earth Scenes, 18 (inset); Krafft-Explorer/Photo Researchers, 21, 27 (bottom right), 50, 51, 53; Tom Stack & Assoc./H. Simon, 22; Ronald Toms, OSF/Earth Scenes, 25 (top left); Patti Murray/Earth Scenes, 25 (top right, bottom left); Martyn Chillmaid, OSF/Earth Scenes 25 (bottom right); Sydney Thomas/Earth Scenes, 27 (top left); Walter H. Hodge/Peter Arnold, Inc., 27 (top right); John Arango/Photo Researchers, 27 (bottom left); Reuters/Bettmann, 28; NASA, 36, 37, 39, 40, 41; USGS, Flagstaff, 38; J. Langevin/Sygma, 43 (top); Sygma, 43 (bottom); Vulcain-Explorer/Photo Researchers, 45; Jacques Jangoux/ Peter Arnold, Inc., 46; Tom McHugh/Photo Researchers, 47; David Weintraub/Photo Researchers, 52.

Library of Congress Cataloging-in-Publication Data

Vogt, Gregory.
Volcanoes/Greg Vogt.
p. cm. (A First book)
Includes bibliographical references and index.
Summary: A study of how volcanoes develop and the effects of their eruptions on Earth. Also discusses famous volcanic eruptions.
ISBN 0-531-20151-1
0-531-15667-2 (paperback)
1. Volcanoes—Juvenile literature. [1. Volcanoes.] I. Title.
II. Series.
QE521.3.V63 1993
551.2'1—dc20 92-23292 CIP AC

CONTENTS

9 Introduction

Chapter One
13 What Are Volcanoes?

Chapter Two
20 Volcanoes Build the Land

Chapter Three
30 Where are the Volcanoes?

Chapter Four
42 Video Research

55 Conclusion

57 Glossary

60 For Further Reading

61 Index

DEDICATION

This book is written in fond remembrance
of Michael David McGarry ("Uncle David").
Gone long ago but not forgotten.

Ruins of St. Pierre, Martinique, after the eruption of Mount Pelée.

INTRODUCTION

Poor August Ciparis. He must have considered himself the unluckiest man in all of the town of Saint-Pierre on the Caribbean island of Martinique. He had done some bad things and had been sent to jail. His jail was a dark dungeon and the only sunlight he saw came through a small window above the door. But on the morning of May 8, 1902, Ciparis was not unlucky. Something terrible was about to happen and his dungeon was the safest place in Saint-Pierre to be.

Four miles from Saint-Pierre, Mount Pelée, a volcanic mountain, exploded with a thunderous eruption. It blasted out huge glowing clouds of hot volcanic ash. One of those clouds raced downslope to Saint-Pierre in just two and a half minutes. The red hot cloud engulfed the town, causing it to explode into a great inferno of fire. Hours later, the town and its 28,000 residents had been reduced to a smoking rubble pile. Everyone was dead except August Ciparis. During the eruption, hot ash flashed into his cell through the window and burned his skin but the dungeon walls protected him from the worst heat. Four days later, rescuers freed him from the cell and treated his injuries. For the rest of his life,

Mount Pelée explodes, as rendered by an artist (top), and in a 1902 photograph (bottom). A newspaper headline described the eruption as "The Most Stupendous and Disastrous Tragedy of Modern Times."

August Ciparis traveled with a circus, making a living by telling his story and showing his scars.

Across the world in another time, another island mountain exploded. The island was Krakatau in Sunda Strait not far from the Indonesian island of Java. The year was 1883.

For most of three months, the mountain had been spouting out ash clouds. But on August 26, the mountain began exploding. One explosion followed another and soon a huge black cloud rose 17 miles (27 km) over the island. The crew of a passing ship were terrified by what they saw and heard. They frantically shoveled overboard heavy mounds of ash that threatened to sink their ship. On another passing ship, nearly half the crew had their eardrums smashed by the sounds of the eruptions.

The Krakatau eruption continued for twenty-one hours and then suddenly stopped just before 10:00 A.M. on August 27. But the real show was about to begin. A few minutes later, a part of the mountain blew up and then much of it collapsed into the hole created by the eruption. Ash and gas shot skyward many tens of miles. In seconds, nearly the entire mountain was gone. A huge sea wave (the largest of many) spread outward and crashed on the surrounding island coastlines. Entire towns were erased and more than 30,000 people were killed. When the eruption stilled and the smoke cleared, most of the island of Krakatau was gone.

Earth presently has more than six hundred active volcanoes that could erupt at any time. Some are very dangerous, like the volcanoes on Krakatau and Martinique. Their explosions devastate the land, sometimes for hundreds of miles around. Other volcanoes, such as those on the island of Hawaii, are relatively safe. They spray out large fountains of molten lava that sometimes flow down to the sea. Lava reaching the sea becomes new island rock so that the island grows with each eruption.

Many volcanoes are found on islands but others are found on the continents. North America has Mount Saint Helens in the state of Washington. It erupted in 1980. Nearby are Mount Ranier and Mount Lassen. Mexico has El Chichón and Parícutin. Europe's Italy has Etna and Vesuvius. Still other volcanoes exist beneath the sea. Lava, upwelling from ocean floor cracks mounds up and sometimes climbs above the water to become islands.

Volcanoes are important to life on Earth. While a volcano may kill us if we get too close during an eruption, volcanoes also do good things for us. Long ago, shortly after Earth was created, much of the surface of our planet bubbled and steamed as though the Earth was one giant volcano. As it cooled, it became solid. Gases that seeped out became our atmosphere. When the atmosphere became cool enough, water vapor condensed into rain, turning low spots into oceans and lakes. Everything we see on Earth today—trees, soil, rivers, automobiles, and houses—was once part of the molten material of Earth's volcanic past. Volcanoes are important. Just what are they? How do they work? Where do they come from? What do they do?

1

WHAT ARE VOLCANOES?

The Hawaiian Islands were created by volcanoes. Hot lava, spewing out from cracks in the Pacific Ocean floor, laid down layer upon layer of lava rock. Over millions of years, the lava mounded up and poked above the waves to become islands. The highest point on Hawaii, the biggest of the Hawaiian Islands, is more than 13,000 feet (3,962 m) above sea level. But when you measure from the ocean floor, it is taller than Mount Everest.

Hawaii is actually made up of five volcanoes. The tallest volcano is Mauna Loa but the most active is Kilauea. In fact, Kilauea is one of the most active volcanoes in the world. In a six-year period, beginning with an eruption that started in 1983, Kilauea spilled out enough lava to pave a highway that could circle Earth four times. Its rivers of lava have flooded more than 23 square miles (59.56 sq. km) of land and poured into the ocean, adding one hundred acres (40.47 hectares) of new land to the island. Many homes have been destroyed by the lava, but Kilauea, for all its eruptive activity, is a fairly safe volcano. There is a golf course near the volcano's summit and people continue to live on its flanks even when it is erupting. It is only when its

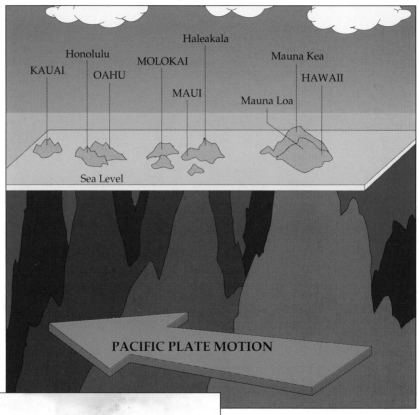

KAUAI
Honolulu
OAHU
MOLOKAI
Haleakala
MAUI
Mauna Kea
HAWAII
Mauna Loa
Sea Level

PACIFIC PLATE MOTION

(top) The Hawaiian Islands, volcanic mountains rising from the ocean floor, are a result of plate tectonic movement. (left) Lava spouts from Kilauea in Hawaii.

river of lava begins heading for homes that people get out of the way.

Merapi, a 9,500-foot (2,896-m) high peak on the Indonesian island of Java is a different kind of volcano. It may be one of the world's most dangerous volcanoes. In the last thousand years, it has erupted more than sixty times. It is capable of belching out red hot streams of lava and huge clouds of ash that can spread 40 miles (64.4 km) away. Glowing avalanches of hot rock can roll down its sides at speeds of more than a mile a minute. It shoots out large bombs of sticky lava that fly through the air like cannon balls. Tropical rains will mix with ash piles left by eruptions to become unstoppable mud flows that flood down the mountain sweep up anything in its path. An eruption of Merapi in 1930 killed 1,300 people. Scientists, who are studying the mountain, think a much bigger eruption is inevitable. The entire mountain top could explode.

Why are Kilauea and Merapi so different? Part of the answer has to do with the kind of molten lava each is created from. Before going further it is important to understand what volcanoes are and how they form.

A *volcano* is a mountain that is formed in a special way. Many of Earth's mountains, like the Rocky Mountain chain, are formed by folding or crumpling of the edges of the Earth's continents as they slowly move about. Others have been carved out by erosion after the land has been uplifted. Volcanoes, however, are different. They create themselves. Molten lava from deep within the Earth finds its way to the surface through cracks. As the lava gushes or is blasted out, it accumulates in piles. The piles grow and eventually become the mountain. The crack through which the lava flows out is called a *vent,* and most volcanoes are built from many vents through many thousands of years.

Some volcanoes, such as Mount Fuji in Japan, form very steep and picturesque mountains. Others spread out and have very gentle slopes. These volcanoes look almost like giant shields when seen from above. The shape of the volcano is determined largely by the kind of lava that makes it up.

Lava is molten rock, or rock that has melted. On Kilauea, the hottest lavas that erupt from its vents are almost 2,200° F (1,204° C). Lava this hot is white. As it is exposed to the air, the molten lava begins to cool and its color changes. At 2,000° F (1,093° C) it is yellow, and at 1,650° F (899° C) it is orange. As it continues to cool, lava turns bright red at 1,290° F (699° C) and dull red when it is about 930° F (499° C). Finally, the lava becomes solid and turns black, dark red, or grey in color. Depending on many factors, including how fast the lava cooled, it may be glassy in texture, rough and chunky, smooth and ropy, or even frothy with millions of tiny bubbles.

Molten lava is usually made up of silica (the elements oxygen and silicon) and a variety of other elements such as aluminum, magnesium, sodium, potassium, and iron. Lavas that are very rich in silica, sodium, and potassium are thick and pasty. Lavas that are rich in iron and magnesium tend to be runny, almost like hot taffy.

Another important part of lava is dissolved gases such as water, sulfur dioxide, and carbon dioxide. It is the gases in lava that propel the lava as it nears the Earth's surface. It happens something like the way a soda pop can rush out of a bottle. Carbon dioxide gas, the fizz, is dissolved in the liquid when the cap is on. With the cap removed, the gas expands into bubbles. If you place your thumb over the top and shake the bottle, so much gas is released that it propels the soda pop out of the bottle, causing an eruption. Lava beneath Earth's surface is under great pressure from the millions of tons of rock above it. The gases in the lava remain dissolved. But if an earthquake occurs, cracks in the rock may reach all the way to the surface. If this happens, the pressure is released. The dissolved gases expand, propelling the lava to the surface.

This 1984 photograph of the eruption of Mauna Loa shows a lava tube near a vent at an altitude of 9,400 feet (2,865 m).

Lava spews and flows.

Because some kinds of lava are thin and runny, the expanding gases will cause the lava to gush out of the vent like a geyser. Molten lava will spray upward hundreds of feet into the air. The thin lava will collect in large lava lakes and form slow moving rivers that will spread the lava out over the land. Gradually, a broad and gently sloping volcano will build up.

Thick lava, on the other hand, will rise sluggishly to the surface. The gas will have more difficulty escaping from the liquid and will actually explode the lava into small fragments. The fragments fall as ash nearby and form steep-sided cones. Sometimes, the sticky lava will clog the vent so that no more can escape. In time, the pressure below will become so great that the cone will swell. Finally, when the weight of the ground can no longer contain the pressure, the volcano explodes. The explosion may be so great that the entire mountain top is blasted away.

There is one more important question to ask here about volcanoes. Where does the heat come from? There is no easy answer to this question and scientists are still looking for evidence to explain where the heat comes from. It may be that there are several sources of heat. The heat could be left over from the formation of the Earth more than 4.5 billion years ago. The heat could come from the decay of radioactive elements in the Earth's interior. Another possible source of the heat is the friction produced as the gravity of the Earth and Moon tug on each other. Still another possible source of the heat is the friction of large continental masses of Earth's crust rubbing against each other. For the time being, many scientists believe radioactive decay of elements to be the strongest contributor to volcanic heat. The answer, however, could change as scientists continue their studies.

2

VOLCANOES BUILD THE LAND

Earth's surface is constantly being assaulted by slow but powerful forces. Wind, rain, ice, natural chemicals, and even animals combine together to wear away rock into soil. The soil is carried away by rivers and dropped into the oceans. In time, huge mountain ranges are worn down into rolling hills and broad planes. In time, Grand Canyons are carved.

If erosion was the only force affecting Earth's surface, the land from all the continents would eventually be spread out on the ocean floor. The name of our planet would have to be changed from "Earth" to planet "Water." Fortunately, erosion isn't the only force affecting Earth. Volcanic action is another force, and most of the time it does exactly the opposite of erosion. It creates new land. In 1943, a crack opened in a pit in a Mexican farmer's cornfield. A strong spray of volcanic ash and cinders shot up into the air and later molten lava flowed out to cover surrounding land. In a few months, the nearby town of Parícutin was destroyed by the lava. Two years later another town, San Juan Parangaricutiro, was inundated by lava as well. All that was spared was a church tower. By the end of its eruption in

Parícutin, Mexico. The tremendous volcano erupted from 1943 to 1952, consuming several towns.

The birth of the island of Surtsey, which appeared near Iceland as a volcano and erupted for more than three years.

Surtsey as it looks today.

1952, the cornfield had changed into a 1,650-foot (503-m) mountain.

In late 1963, a cook on a fishing boat off the south coast of Iceland spotted a cloud of dark smoke rising from the ocean. The smoke signaled the birth of a new volcanic island. The eruption had actually begun weeks or months before as volcanic lava poured out from the ocean floor to form a conical mound. The mound eventually piled high enough to poke above the ocean waves. In successive eruptions that lasted three-and-a-half years, a new island, Surtsey, was born. It wasn't long before plants and animals found their way to the island and called it home.

Parícutin and the island of Surtsey are just two of the many Earth landforms that were created by volcanoes. Many volcanoes, such as the 14,377-foot (4,382-m) Mount Ranier in the state of Washington, are much bigger than Parícutin and Surtsey. But all volcanoes have one thing in common, they were each constructed of rock, cinders, and ash that was once molten rock from the Earth's interior.

Volcanoes create many products. Rock is one of the most important of these products. In the previous chapter, two different kinds of lava were discussed. Thick and pasty lavas that are very rich in the elements of silica, sodium, and potassium, and runny lavas that are rich in iron and magnesium. Each kind of lava produces its own kinds of rocks.

Thick, slow-moving lava produces chunky, jagged lava rock that is known by the Hawaiian name of *aa* (pronounced ah-ah). The rock is porous from gas bubbles trapped inside as it cooled. Broken surfaces of aa are jagged. You would not like to fall down on it. The runny lavas produce a much smoother surface. Next time a cake is being baked, watch what happens when the batter is being poured into the cake pan. Ripples form at the surface of the batter as it flows to the edges of the pan. The surface of runny lava will quickly cool to form a crust and the ripples in it will harden. This rock is given by the Hawaiian name *pahoehoe* (pronounced pa-hoy-hoy). Often, pahoehoe has so many ripples in it, it looks like a large pile of coiled heavy ropes.

Other rock types are also created by volcanoes. One is a very glassy black rock called *obsidian.* Obsidian cools so quickly that the elements that are found in the lava don't have time to get organized and grow into microscopic

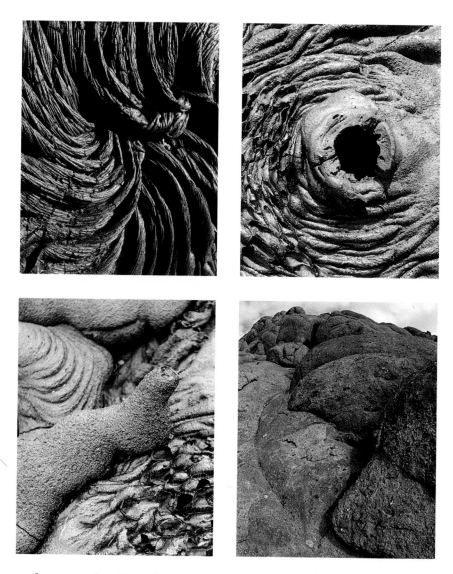

A menagerie of lava flows: pahoehoe, which looks like rope (top left); "glassy" lava (bottom left); "pillow" lava (bottom right); and a combination of glassy and ropey lava forming around a gas bubble (top right).

crystals. Instead, they just freeze where they are and become glass. Small droplike globs of obsidian that freeze in mid-air as they are blasted out of a volcano are sometimes polished for jewelry. They are called *pele's tears.* If lava is frothy with gas bubbles and it cools very quickly, it may take on the appearance of a sponge. This rock is called *pumice,* and it may have so much air trapped inside that it can actually float on water.

The lava and cinders ejected by volcanoes onto Earth's surface pile up to form volcanic mountains. Four main kinds of volcanoes are formed. Most volcanoes take cone shapes, something like the way sand poured from your hands on a beach forms a cone. If the lava is sticky and stiff, the cone will be fairly steep-sided. The slopes of Mount Fuji, in Japan, are angled at about thirty degrees. Mount Fuji is called a *composite* volcano because it is built up of mixed layers of cinders and lava flows. Mauna Loa, in Hawaii, is a *shield volcano* that is made up of layer upon layer of runny lava flows. Its slopes at an angle of only about six degrees. If an eruption consists mainly of cinders, a steep-side *cinder cone* forms. The fourth kind of volcano is called a *lava dome.* Domes are formed from lava that is so sticky that it hardly flows at all. Instead, the lava bulges up to form a large, rounded pile of very rough lava rock.

Another category of products volcanoes produce are solid particles called *pyroclastics.* Pyroclastics can be any size from as small as dust on up to house-sized blocks, but all have been thrown into the air. The finest particles, about as fine as flour, are called *dust.* Gritty rice-sized particles are called *ash* and rough rocky particles about the size of golf balls are called *blocks.* The exceptions are *volcanic*

Volcanoes take many shapes: Hawaii's Mauna Loa, a shield volcano (top left); Japan's Mount Fuji, a composite volcano (top right); Peru's El Misti, a cinder cone (bottom left); and Japan's Asama, featuring a lava dome (bottom right).

bombs that are sticky globs of lava, the size of footballs and larger, that are blasted out during an eruption and streak across the sky. While still in mid-air, they partially cool into a rounded shape.

Pyroclastics are very important volcanic products because they pile up to create rich and fertile new soil for growing crops. But, in the short term, pyroclastics can be real problems. During the 1991 eruption of Mount Pinatubo in the Philippines, the volcano put out huge quantities of ash that settled over the surrounding countryside. Nearby was the 50,000-acre (20,235-hectare) Clark Air Base. For ninety years, the United States had leased the land on which the base was built from the Philippine government. The

Ash from Mount Pinatubo piles in the streets of Olongapo, Philippines.

volcano's ash fall all but buried the base, collapsing many buildings under its weight. Because of the massive expense of cleanup and rebuilding required to reopen the base, as well as a changing political scene in the Philippines, the United States returned control of the land to the Philippine government.

Messing up Clark Air Base wasn't all that Pinatubo did. The volcano kicked up large quantities of pyroclastics into the atmosphere that hung there for many months. There was so much dust that Space Shuttle astronaut crews orbiting Earth complained about the poor views they were having of the ground.

Although Mount Pinatubo's eruption was one of this century's largest, larger eruptions are known in history and far larger eruptions have been found in the prehistoric geological record. In 1815, the volcanic mountain of Tambora in the Indonesian island chain self-destructed in a tremendous eruption. One-third of the mountain was gone and thousands of people perished in the eruption or died shortly afterwards in the devastation it created in Indonesia. But Tambora's damage was not restricted to Indonesia. The dust it spewed into the atmosphere is believed to have altered Earth's climate for a year. The dust reflected some of the Sun's warmth and dropped Earth surface temperatures. The next year was referred to as the "year with no summer." People in New England had to wear warm coats during the summer and early frosts in August hurt crop production. The crop loss was especially damaging in Europe where food was in short supply because of the Napoleanic Wars.

3

WHERE ARE THE VOLCANOES?

Long ago when the Sun, Earth, and all the other planets first formed, our solar system was a messy place. Earth was still a hot sphere of melted rock. Left over were many pieces of rock and metal like the asteroids and meteoroids of today's solar system. As the Earth and the other planets orbited their new sun, their gravities attracted these leftover bodies and pulled them in. Each collision generated heat that kept Earth and the other three inner planets, Mercury, Venus, and Mars, in a liquid state.

In time the debris began to be swept up and collisions became less and less common. Earth's surface started cooling, and when it did it began forming a hard crust. The crust was brittle and it broke in many places. Along the cracks, hot lava welled up to form volcanoes. The whole planet was covered with these volcanoes. With each eruption, much heat was released back into space and the planet continued to cool. Dissolved gas in the lava was also released and it collected around Earth to form an atmosphere.

The cooling continued. When the atmosphere cooled below the boiling point of water, 212° F (100° C), water vapor condensed to form clouds. Eventually, rains came, helping the surface to cool even more. The volcanic eruption rate diminished and water collected in large pools that grew into lakes and oceans. Although our atmosphere and oceans are very different today from what they were like back then, they owe their existence to volcanic eruptions.

Volcanoes are far less common today than they were in Earth's early history. Where are they located?

In the United States, active volcanoes are found near the western coast in California, Washington, and Alaska. Inactive volcanoes and the weathered cores of extinct volcanoes are found in Arizona, Utah, Nevada, Idaho, Colorado, Wyoming, Montana, and Oregon. The state of Hawaii owes its existence to cluster of volcanoes that grew above Pacific Ocean floor.

Crossing the northern Pacific Ocean we find many volcanoes along the eastern coast in Kamchatka (Russia), Japan, the Philippines, New Guinea, and New Zealand. On the southern end of South America, we again find volcanoes. Like volcanoes in the United States, the volcanoes of South America and the Central American countries to the north lie along the western coasts. If you mark the locations of today's active volcanoes on a map, you will make an interesting discovery. Many of the world's volcanoes form a ring that surrounds the Pacific Ocean!

Another clustering of volcanoes extends between the continents of Europe and Africa. The path eventually crosses the length of Indonesia and joins with the Pacific ring at New Guinea. By mapping volcanoes, scientists can tell that volcanoes do not occur randomly, but follow a pattern. What causes the pattern? It took many decades of

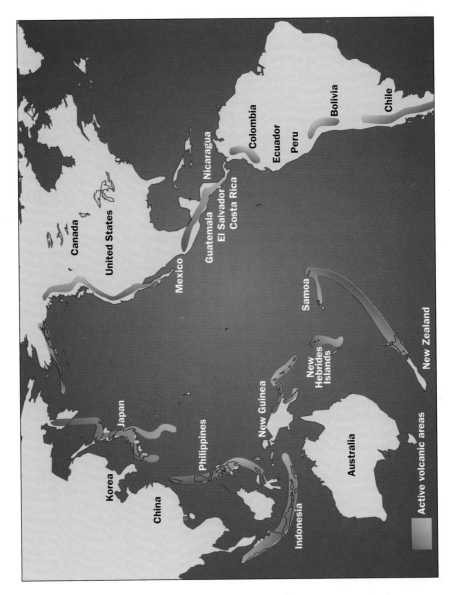

This map shows the Pacific volcanic rim or the " Ring of Fire."

intensive scientific research to begin to untangle a giant jigsaw puzzle of clues and piece them together to form a picture.

Some of the most important clues were found in the middle of the Atlantic Ocean. Careful mapping surveys discovered a submarine mountain chain running the entire length of the ocean from the Arctic to Antarctic circles. More remarkably, the ridge was positioned almost exactly between the surrounding continents. It followed the shorelines! Scientists named the chain the *Mid-Atlantic Ridge.*

In the center of the mountain chain, scientists discovered trenches. When they lowered scoops on cables to collect rocks from the trenches, they discovered the rocks were volcanic and not very old. When they repeated the sampling on the eastern and western sides of the ridge, they again found volcanic rocks, but the rocks were much older. What was happening?

These discoveries and many others from all over the Earth eventually led to a new idea called *plate tectonics.* If we could slice our Earth in half, we would see that its interior is something like the inside of an egg. In the center of the Earth is a heavy *core* of metals (yoke). It is surrounded by a thick layer of almost liquid rock called the *mantle* (egg white). To the outside is the rocky *crust* that we live on (shell). Compared to the rest of the Earth, the crust is thin. It ranges anywhere from possibly 5-miles (8-km) thick under parts of the oceans to about 40-miles (64.4-km) thick in mountainous areas of the continents.

Plate tectonics means that the Earth's crust is broken in many places to form a series of about twenty gigantic

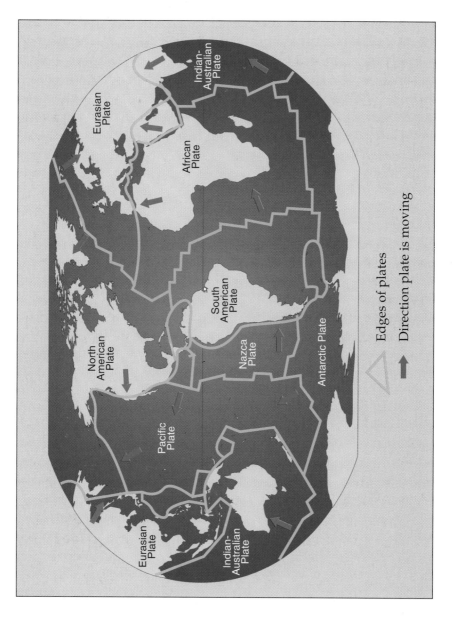

Plate Tectonics map.

plates. The plates match up to each other like pieces of a jigsaw puzzle. But the puzzle is moving. The North American, Caribbean, and the South American Plates are slowly moving westward at a rate of about a couple of inches per year. Across the Atlantic Ocean, Eurasia is moving very slowly to the southwest and Africa is rotating counterclockwise. The driving force behind the movement of these plates is the volcanic pressure along the Mid-Atlantic ridge. Hot lava is slowly being forced up in the area of the trench and the plates are being pushed apart.

Each of these plates is moving with the uppermost part of the Earth's mantle. The underlying mantle is also in motion. At the middle on the other side of Earth, they run into other plates. The collision has caused the plates to crumple like the front ends of cars that run into each other. The plate under the Pacific Ocean, being thinner than the continental plates, is driven downward. The continental plate piles on top.

The result of all this movement is that the rim of the Pacific Ocean is very mountainous. Earthquakes are common and hot lava may travel up cracks to the surface to make volcanoes.

Scientists have created maps of the world that show the location of the tectonic plates. On those same maps, they plotted active volcanoes and earthquakes. The pattern is clear. The majority of the world's volcanoes and earthquakes occur where tectonic plates come together.

With the coming of the Space Age, scientists learned that Earth isn't the only world with volcanoes. Robot spacecraft sent by the National Aeronautics and Space

Administration to Venus, Mars, and Jupiter have each discovered volcanoes. Astronauts walking on the Moon have returned home with volcanic rocks.

Several spacecraft missions to Mars in the 1970s helped scientists create maps of the Martian surface. They found broad lava planes and several giant volcanoes. One of those volcanoes, Mons Olympus, is more than twice the height of Mount Everest on Earth and its base is more than

Lunar volcanic rock.

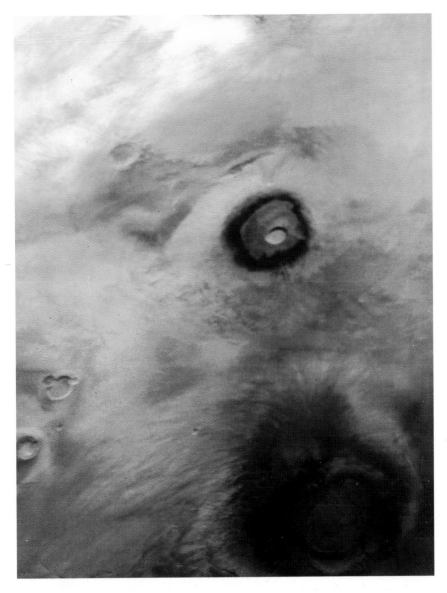

Volcanic activity on the planet Mars, as seen from the Viking I spacecraft.

three hundred miles wide. The spacecraft did not find signs of recent volcanic activity on Mars but they only collected data for a few years. Many Earth volcanoes lie dormant for decades before erupting again.

The Voyager spacecraft that traveled to the outer giant planets also made a volcanic discovery. Jupiter's moon Io (pronounced eye-oh) has several active volcanoes that were spewing out large quantities of sulfur compounds when Voyager flew by.

A Viking I photograph of Mars's Mons Olympus.

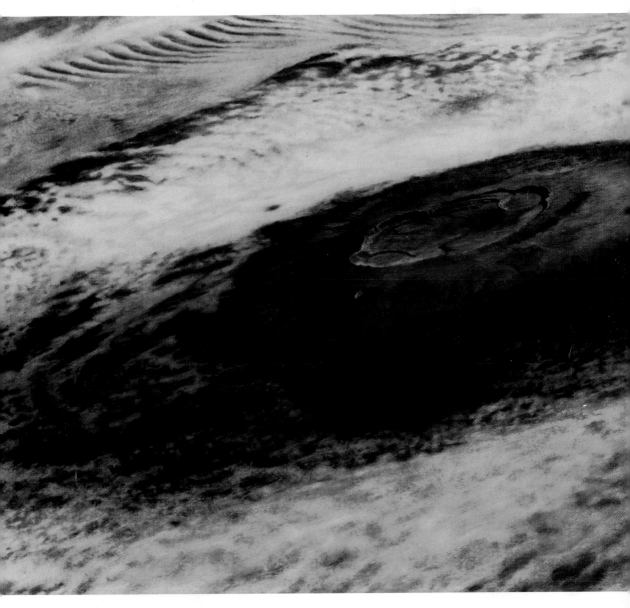

Artist's rendition of Mons Olympus.

More recently, the Magellan mission to Venus used radar waves to map the surface of Venus through its dense cloud cover. The pictures it sent back to Earth in 1990 revealed that Venus is loaded with volcanoes of all sizes and shapes. Some of the volcanoes show signs of recent lava flows.

Volcanic explosion on Jupiter's satellite, Io.

Volcanic mountain on Io.

4

VOLCANO RESEARCH

Kagoshima is a very special city in Japan. Its half of a million people live right across a bay from the very active Mount Sakurajima volcano. It is one of the world's most active volcanoes and has had thousands of small explosive eruptions since they began to be recorded in A.D. 708. Since 1955, Sakurajima has been erupting with frequent falls of cinders and smoke. The debris from the volcano is irritating, but the people who live nearby Kagoshima have learned to live with the volcano. Children wear bright yellow hard hats to protect their heads as they go to school. Everyone bathes frequently to get rid of the dust and cars never stay clean. But life goes on.

In the Colombian town of Armero, life didn't go on. On November 13, 1985, the Nevada del Ruíz volcano began erupting. The last time it had erupted was in 1845. The volcano seemed to be safe, but it wasn't. By evening, red-hot ash and cinders boiled up from the volcano's crater and poured over the ice cap in fiery rivers. The heat melted part of the mountaintop's ice cap. Water mixed with soil and rumbled down the mountain in great waves of mud. The mud poured into local rivers and mixed with their waters.

These pictures show the massive mudslide that hit Armero after a volcanic eruption.

The Lagunillas river was already overflowing from the previous week's heavy rains. It became a wall of muddy water that raced down the river valley at speeds of up to 25 mph (40 kmph). At the outside of a sweeping river bend 30 miles (48 km) from the mountain, lay the city of Aero. Many of Aero's residents were in bed when the torrent of mud smashed into the town. By the next day, the extent of the tragedy became apparent. Aero was destroyed. More than five thousand homes in the region were damaged or destroyed. Twenty-two thousand people were buried by the mud and another ten thousand were injured.

Millions of people live near volcanoes. Some, such as Sakurajima in Japan, are relatively safe even when erupting and others are very dangerous. Which is which? Even more important, how can we predict when dangerous volcanoes will erupt again so that people can evacuate to safety?

A *volcanologist* is a scientist who specializes in volcanoes and tries to answer these questions and many more. Volcanologists go to college and study many subjects to prepare them for their work. They study chemistry, physics, biology, geology, mathematics, English, and foreign languages. They learn how to operate scientific instruments and how to design their own instruments. They study research techniques including how to read aerial photographs and satellite pictures. Their studies are exciting and challenging and take them around the world to study volcanoes in action, those that recently erupted, and those that erupted long ago.

When a volcano is selected for study, the volcanologist knows that there isn't another one exactly like it in the whole world. Volcanologists have many objectives in studying a

A volcanologist uses a chromograph to measure gases.

particular volcano. There is curiosity to know the unknown. There is a need to understand how the volcano operates. What is its structure inside? What kinds of lava does it produce? How much dissolved gas does it have?

Because it is not possible to go deep into the Earth to study volcanoes from the inside, volcanologists use a variety of tools to measure them from the surface. One of the best tools available is a *seismometer*. Seismometers are devices that measure the vibrations produced by earthquakes.

Volcanologists examine the impact site where a volcanic bomb has hit the ground.

A seismometer showing minor tremors.

Volcanologists have learned that movements of lava within volcanoes crack rock and cause many tremors that can be felt on the surface with sensitive instruments. With several seismometers working together from different locations, the exact depth and location of the lava movements can be plotted on a map. This information can be very useful. In Hawaii, for example, hundreds or even thousands of small quakes over a period of several weeks usually means an eruption is due to happen.

Another good tool for a volcanologist is a *tilt meter.* Tilt meters measure very slow movements of land by seeing how their surface angles change. Many volcanoes signify that something is happening by swelling. Their insides begin filling with lava, and the lava slowly expands the land surface. The swelling may be too slow to be seen, but tilt meters can detect it. Imagine baking a cake with an uninflated balloon inside. Then imagine what would happen to the surface of the cake if you could slowly blow the balloon up. The same thing happens to volcanoes inflating with lava. If the swelling is proceeding rapidly, an eruption could be soon. If the tiltmeters detect the volcano is getting smaller, the volcano may be entering a quiet period.

Seismometers, tilt meters, chemical tests, and even electrical and magnetic studies of volcanoes are just some of the tools of the volcanologist. When all the clues are assembled, forecasts of what may happen can be made.

An electronic tiltmeter is buried by falling tephra, the solid material that falls to the ground during volcanic eruptions.

A volcanologist reads a seismometer.

These forecasts are based on percentages. The only time a volcanologist says that there is a one hundred percent chance of an eruption is when a volcano is erupting. Otherwise, the forecast is less precise. The forecast might be that there is a ten percent chance the volcano will erupt over the next several weeks. Longer range forecasts can be stated with more certainty.

Another important element necessary in forecasting volcanic activity involves careful field work. This work is done by volcanologists who piece together the history of the volcano through the study of its past deposits. Field work is

Obtaining lava samples can be hot, dangerous work.

Volcanologists witness the violent drama of an exploding volcano.

The spectacular 1980 eruption of Mount Saint Helens, Washington.

not as glamorous and exciting as the technological tools, but it is as important. Through careful field work, two volcanologists very familiar with Mount Saint Helens in Washington state predicted in 1978 that an eruption of the mountain was likely before the end of the century. Their prediction was based partly on geological studies of its previous eruptions over the past 4,500 years. The scientists could see that the mountain was due for another eruption. Mount Saint Helens cooperated and blew up two years later!

Part of the aftermath of Mount Saint Helens—forests for miles around were devastated.

When a volcano erupts, something important happens. The volcano changes. The volcano may be larger or smaller than it was before the eruption. Earthquakes will have created new cracks inside. Lava flows and cinder piles will have changed its surface. All this means that the volcano is different from what it was before. And that means the volcanologists studying the volcano have to go back and figure out what those changes mean to the volcano's future eruptions. The work of a volcanologist is a never-ending challenge. But it is a career that offers great rewards. One of the rewards is the satisfaction gained by making new discoveries and contributing to our total knowledge of one of the most dramatic processes in nature. Another is learning enough about individual volcanoes to enable accurate eruption forecasts to be made. An accurate forecast could save thousands of lives!

CONCLUSION

We have learned much about the volcanoes that dot our planet. We know that molten rock beneath the surface is under great pressure. As continents slowly move on great plates earthquakes are created. The cracks they produce provide pathways for lava to reach the surface. Lava, cinders, ash, and dust mound up around the surface opening and may eventually grow to become a large mountain. We have also learned that volcanologists have come a long way in understanding volcanic eruptions. In some places their studies have led to reliable eruption forecasts that saved many lives.

Although only a small number of volcanoes are active today, we know that all of Earth's rock, soil, water, and atmosphere were born in the molten material that was Earth after our solar system came into being. Even as land and mountains were being created, erosion was wearing them away and recycling them into soil and new rock. Eventually, plants took hold, used the soil, water, and atmosphere for growth and greened the surface of the land. Animals ate the plants and they grew too. As they died, plants and animals recycled, just as rock and soil, only much faster.

Today, the recycling continues. Volcanoes create new land and erosion, and living things recycle it. What you may not have thought of is that you are a part of that recycling. Although you may live in a part of the world where there are no active volcanoes, you are still closely related to them. Every atom in your body was once inside the earth. Volcanoes brought your atoms to the surface to be recycled into you!

GLOSSARY

Aa — A crusty lava composed of jagged, angular blocks.

Ash — Volcanic particles about the size of a grain of rice.

Bombs — Football-sized globs of molten lava tossed out of a volcano that harden before they hit the ground.

Cinder cone — A steep-sided volcano cone comprised of cinders.

Cinders — Golf ball sized particles ejected by volcanoes.

Composite volcano — A steep-sided volcano cone formed of mixed layers of ash and lava.

Core — The innermost layer of the Earth composed mainly of metals.

Crust — The outermost layer of the Earth composed mainly of rocks.

Dust — Fine, powder-like particles.

Lava — Molten rock on the surface of the Earth. Lava is also used to refer to rock formed when lava hardens.

Lava dome — A dome-shaped crusty plug of lava that blocks the vent of a volcano. With continued pressure from underneath, the dome expands in all directions.

Mantle — The middle layer of the Earth composed mainly of very hot rock that is plasticlike.

Mid-Atlantic Ridge — Mountain chain running down the middle of the Atlantic Ocean floor.

Obsidian — Volcanic glass.

Pahoehoe — A runny lava that hardens with a ropy surface.

Pele's tears — Small, tear-shaped polished pieces of obsidian.

Plate tectonics — Large continent-sized rafts of the Earth's crust that float on the mantle.

Pumice — A grayish, glass rock filled with bubble holes and usually light enough to float on water.

Pyroclastic — Volcanic material (ash, cinders, bombs, and so on) that has been explosively ejected from the volcano's vent.

Seismometer — A device for measuring earthquake vibrations in the Earth.

Shield volcano — A broad, gently sloping cone formed from repeated eruptions of runny lava.

Tilt meter — A volcano measurement tool that tells volcanologists when a volcano is expanding or contracting.

Vent — The path in a volcano through which magma travels to the surface.

Volcano — A vent or crack in the surface of the Earth through which lava flows out and the mountain that builds up about it.

Volcanologist — A scientist who specializes in the study of volcanoes.

FOR FURTHER READING

Bramwell, Martyn. *Earth Science Library: Volcanoes and Earthquakes.*
    London: Franklin Watts, 1986.

Jennings, Terry. *Exploring Our World: Volcanoes and Earthquakes.*
    Freeport, NY: Marshall Cavendish, 1989.

Lauber, Patricia. *Volcano, The Eruption and Healing of Mount St. Helens.*
    New York: Bradbury Press, 1986.

Fradin, Dennis B. *Disaster! Volcanoes.* Chicago: Childrens Press,
    1982.

Krafft, M. *Volcanoes.* Milwaukee: Raintree Publishers, 1988.

Radlauer, Ruth. *Volcanoes.* Chicago: Childrens Press, 1981.

Vogt, Gregory. *Predicting Volcanic Eruptions.* New York:
    Franklin Watts, 1989.

INDEX

Aa, 24
Aero (Colombia), 44
Alaska, 31
Aluminum, 16
Arizona, 31
Armero (Columbia), 42
Ash, 15, 26, 29, 55
Asteroids, 30
Atlantic Ocean, 33, 35
Atmosphere, 30

Blocks, 26
Bombs, 15, 28

California, 31
Carbon dioxide, 16
Caribbean Plate, 35
Central America, 31
Cinders, 55
Ciparis, August, 9–11
Clark Air Base, 28, 29
Colorado, 31
Continents, 20
Core, 35
Crust, 30, 35

Dust, 26

El Chichón, 12
Erosion, 20

Gases, 12, 16–17, 30

Hawaii, 12, 13, 26, 31, 47

Iceland, 23
Idaho, 31
Indonesia, 29
Io, 40
Iron, 16, 24

Japan, 16, 26, 31, 44
Java, 15
Jupiter, 36, 40

Kamchatka (Russia), 31
Kagoshima (Japan), 42
Kilauea, 13, 16
Krakatau, Java, 11

Lagunillas River, 44
Lava, 12–13, 15–19, 26, 30, 41,
    47–48, 55

Magellan, 41
Magnesium, 16, 24

Mantle, 35
Mars, 30, 36, 38
Mauna Loa, 13, 26
Merapi, 15
Mercury, 30
Meteoroids, 30
Mexico, 12
Mid-Atlantic Ridge, 33, 35
Mons Olympus, 38
Montana, 31
Moon, 19, 36
Mount Etna, 12
Mount Everest, 13, 38
Mount Fuji, 16, 26
Mount Lassen, 12
Mount Pelée, 9
Mount Pinatubo, 28–29
Mount Ranier, 12, 24
Mount Saint Helens, 12, 53
Mount Sakurajima, 42, 44
Mount Vesuvius, 12
Mud flows, 15

Napoleanic Wars, 29
National Aeronautics and Space
     Administration, 36
Nevada, 31
Nevada del Ruíz, 42
New Guinea, 31
New Zealand, 31
North American Plate, 35

Obsidian, 24, 26
Oregon, 31

Pacific Ocean, 13, 31, 36
Parícutin, 12, 20, 24
Pele's tears, 26
Philippines, 28, 29, 31

Plate tectonics, 35, 36
Potassium, 16, 24
Pumice, 26
Pyroclastics, 26, 28

Rocky Mountains, 15

Saint-Pierre, Martinique, 9
San Juan Parangaricutiro,
     Mexico, 20
Seismometer, 45
Silica, 16, 24
Sodium, 16, 24
South America, 31
South American Plate, 35
Sulfur dioxide, 16
Sunda Strait, 11
Surtsey, 23–24

Tambora, 29
Tilt meter, 47

Utah, 31

Vent, 15
Venus, 30, 36, 41
Volcanic heat, 19
Volcanoes
     Cinder cone, 26
     Composite, 26
     Lava dome, 26
     Shield, 26
Volcanologist, 44, 50
Volcanologists, 44–47, 50, 54
Voyager, 40

Washington, 24, 31, 53
Wyoming, 31

ABOUT THE AUTHOR

Gregory Vogt is the Crew Educational Affairs Liaison at the NASA Johnson Space Center in Houston, Texas; he has been a science teacher and an educator for NASA for many years. Mr. Vogt is also the author of many children's books and articles on science. His recent books for Franklin Watts include *An Album of Modern Spaceships, Forests on Fire: The Fight to Save Our Trees,* and *Predicting Volcanic Eruptions.* He says he hopes that students who read *Volcanoes* will be inspired to study further and "learn more about the forces at work in and on the Earth."

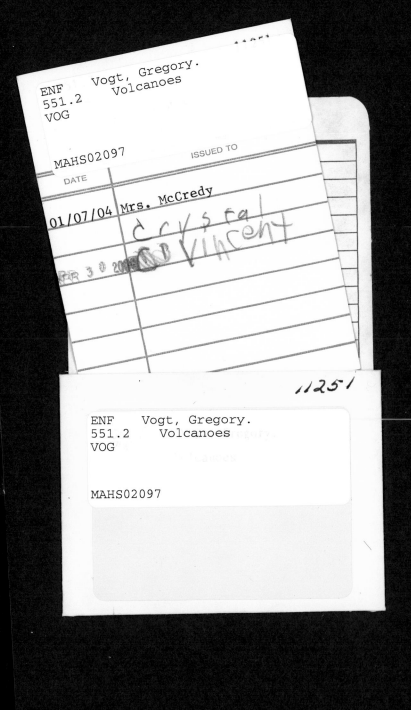

ENF   Vogt, Gregory.
551.2   Volcanoes
VOG

MAHS02097   ISSUED TO

DATE

01/07/04 Mrs. McCredy

Crystal
Vincent

APR 3 0 20

11251

ENF   Vogt, Gregory.
551.2   Volcanoes
VOG

MAHS02097